Reveille for the Soul

Prayers for Military Life

Prayers compiled by
MARGE FENELON

Liguori
Liguori, Missouri

Imprimi Potest:
Thomas D. Picton, C.Ss.R.
Provincial, Denver Province
The Redemptorists

Published by Liguori Publications
Liguori, Missouri 63057-9999

Library of Congress Cataloging-in-Publication Data

Reveille for the soul : prayers for military life : prayers / compiled by
Marge Fenelon. — 1st ed.
    p. cm.
  ISBN 978-0-7648-1878-3
  1. Armed forces —Prayers and devotions. I. Fenelon, Marge.
  BV273.R48 2010
  242'.68 —dc22

                                                    2010011835

Scripture citations are taken from the *New Revised Standard Version
of the Bible*, copyright 1989 by the Division of Christian Education of
the National Council of the Churches of Christ in the USA. All rights
reserved. Used with permission.

Liguori Publications, a nonprofit corporation, is an apostolate of
the Redemptorists. To learn more about the Redemptorists, visit
Redemptorists.com.

To order, call 800-325-9521
www.liguori.org

Printed in the United States of America
14 13 12 11 10   5 4 3 2 1
First Edition

CONTENTS

Hurry Up and Wait—Always in Transition

Look After My Family

Comrades in Arms,
Brothers and Sisters in Our Hearts...

Forever a Servicemember...

HURRY UP AND WAIT— ALWAYS IN TRANSITION

I grew up in a rough section of South Philadelphia, raised in a "blue collar" family with limited money, but lots of love. I have the best parents that anyone could ever have. And because of that, it was very difficult to leave family and friends for the life of an Airman, my true step into "adulthood."

To this day, one of the scariest days of my life began the day I departed for Basic Training. After all, why would anyone in their right mind want to give up everything they love—family, friends, the comfort of the only life they've known their entire young life—to step into a totally new world? A world where they don't know a single soul; are told what to do twenty-four hours a day, seven days a week; and are very far from home!

For most, it's a lifetime of firsts: the first time away from home, first time on a plane, first time relying solely on oneself, and, for some, it is the first time they rely on prayer to help them get through each day. At least that's what I thought. From the moment I arrived at the Military Entrance Processing Station (MEPS), I realized that most of the young men and women I met were just like me—all in search of a better life, a life of service to their nation. Every person has a different "story" about why he or she took this first step to a new life, but I soon realized that none of us would be successful without teamwork; confidence in self and others; faith in those who have been given the responsibility to teach us; and, of course, faith in the Lord. Faith in the Lord can guide us through the most challenging times in our lives.

We rely on faith to get us through each day; on the final day of Basic Training, when we put on the service dress uniform for the first time, are called "Airman," and complete graduation, most of us thank God for giving us the strength to complete the experience and go on to our next challenge. I have been thanking God ever since!

Chief Master Sgt. (Ret.) Kenneth J. McQuiston*

---

* Chief Master Sergeant Kenneth J. McQuiston recently retired as the Command Senior Enlisted Leader of the U.S. Transportation Command at Scott Air Force Base, Illinois, after 28 years of service. As such, he served as the principal advisor to the Combatant Commander for all matters concerning joint force integration, career development, utilization, and sustainment of more than 150,000 enlisted personnel from all branches serving the headquarters and USTRANSCOM's air, land, and sea components throughout the world. Chief McQuiston entered the Air Force in April 1982; after completing basic military training and technical training, he served in various administrative and personnel management positions at squadron, wing, and major command levels. His assignments included command chief master sergeant at the wing, numbered air force, and deployed area of operations supporting "Operation Enduring Freedom" in Afghanistan.

RECRUITING

Dear Lord,
I remember the anxiety I felt the first day I left for basic training.

Missing home, leaving my family, waking up to the unknown at the sound of reveille.

I pray for the armed forces' brand new recruits. Walk with them and give them the strength they will need to adjust to that unknown every day while they shape themselves to become the leaders of tomorrow.

> Staff Sgt. Adam Therrian
> 345th Recruiting Squadron

CHALLENGE AND DIVERSITY

Almighty God,
Today I give you thanks and praise for your continuing presence with me wherever I may be. As the military moves me from place to place, for training and development purposes, thank you for going with me and before me.

There are so many uncertainties, challenges, and changes that come suddenly. Therefore, O God, grant me strength for these transitions, however they come. Help me to be ready and prepared to serve my country and you as I've been called to do.

And Lord, as I learn the military way of life, help me to accept these vastly diverse peoples, places, and requirements. Grant patience to my fellow soldiers and me in the midst of an ever-changing world. As you were faithful to those in the Scriptures, help me to be faithful to you.

Amen.

Chaplain (LTC) David I. Lee
Alabama Army National Guard
226th Area Support Group
Operation Iraqi Freedom, 2003-2004
Camp Arifjan, Kuwait

TRAINING

Eternal God,
Bless our military personnel, both those who lead and those who follow. Guide and protect them in their training, as they prepare to serve within our national and international locations around the globe. Increase their faith in justice, multiply their strength for service, and give them a sense of calm in the midst of constant transitions.

Allow our military men and women to understand that your omnipresence extends to any military base in the world. Let them remember they are an unquestionable asset to our country and our world. Help our men and women in military uniforms to display a confidence-inspiring spirituality, professionalism, and understanding of military life. Direct them to be progressively more effective, and willing to build more bridges, in order to accomplish objectives that are in the best interest of humanity.

Bless their leadership, honor their extensive education, and increase their work responsibilities, so it will clearly convey their dedication toward honor and duty. We ask you, God, to sustain their relationships with their family members who are anxiously and impatiently waiting to physically reunite with them again soon.

We are thankful for the millions of people who have served in our military throughout the generations. May every citizen realize that our country is better and safer because of their valiant efforts.

Thank you, God, for hearing our prayers and for giving us the men and women who serve in our United States military. God, bless the United States of America; God, bless the United States military; God, bless the world.

Chaplain Capt. Ken J. Walden
United States Air Reserves (USAR)
452nd Air Mobility Wing, March Air Reserve Base

COMBAT PREPARATION

The boundary lines have fallen for me in pleasant places; I have a goodly heritage.

Psalm 16:6

Reflection

Yesterday morning I received an e-mail from my oldest son, who is a teacher and the head coach of soccer and baseball at his high school. He said something that struck me as capturing the essence of life's journey: "I really had a great group of horrible athletes this year. We had no talent and excelled." This illustrates an element of boundary lines falling in pleasant places, or "playing the cards one is dealt"—making a choice that becomes either a pleasant or a painful one. For a soccer coach or a commanding general of combat troops, excellence is not always defined by having the finest athletes or the finest combat troops. It is about doing the best you can with who you have. It is about not quitting ever, and finding that making an effort with the people you have makes life pleasant and within these "boundary lines." There is a peace that is unsurpassed and leads to a life of fulfillment—what a "goodly heritage!"

Prayer

Lord of glory, every moment you have given me can be a delight if I will only trust your boundary lines, instead of moving the chalk line because I think I know better.

Amen.

Chaplain Col. Kenneth N. Brown
Multi-National Corps-Iraq

GOD'S WILL

Here I am Lord,
I seek to do your will.
What would you like
for me to do for you today?

Chaplain Col. (Ret.) Leonard F. Stegman
United States Army

MISSION SUCCESS

God of protection and security,
I lift up this prayer as my unit embarks on
a mission. Give me the courage to perform
my duties with the utmost integrity, that
my service might bring credit to myself, my
unit, my country, and ultimately to you, O
God. I willingly put myself in harm's way
in service to my country, in order to protect
our citizens, our allies, and innocent people.
It's my earnest prayer that you grant this
mission success and guarantee the safety of all
servicemembers in my unit. I recognize that
whatever dangers I face, I do not face alone.
My fellow servicemembers are with me, and
you watch over me and inspire me. Help me to
experience your presence and peace in the face
of uncertainty and danger.

Grant wisdom to my commanding officer and to those in authority over me. Guide them to make good decisions, and to take appropriate risks for the sake of the mission. Be with my fellow servicemembers, so that we might work as a team and do our jobs as we have been trained to do. Inspire us, each and every one, to be committed to our mission and to each other.

Bless my family back home and keep them safe. Help them to know that I love them and care for them dearly. Though I am away from them in body, my thoughts are ever with them. As they pray for me, hear their prayers, and answer them.
Amen.

Chaplain Lt. Steven J. Voris
United States Navy

PLANNING

Lord,

Your words to the prophet Jeremiah remind me that you know the plans you have for me. They are plans for me to prosper and not bring me harm, plans to give me "a future with hope" (Jeremiah 29:11). You are the author of time itself. Therefore, you are the great orchestrator of all, and I come before you seeking your wisdom as I set about scheduling the time you've given me and as I enter the planning process.

You know all the tasks that are laid out before me. Some tasks have been assigned to me by others in authority. Other agenda items come from my own heart's desires. For all that is set before me to do and accomplish, I seek your guidance. I seek spiritual discernment to choose judiciously. I pray for insight to schedule and plan activities that will bring you honor and glory. Help me to choose activities that will enrich my life and, more importantly, the lives of others.

Free me from selfish actions that would benefit no one else. Help me to avoid unfruitful endeavors that do nothing to advance your cause. Use me as an instrument of peace even as I am in the profession of arms. Make your will known so that in my life and work, I may ever be your servant. May your Holy Spirit prepare my way. May your presence always guide my footsteps.

I pray this in the name of the one who consulted you in all things, and planned and adjusted his life to your will, Christ our Lord. Amen.

Chaplain Capt. Joseph G. Fisher
48th FW/HC
Royal Air Force Lakenheath, England

Promotion

Almighty God,
As we come together today to celebrate this promotion, we ask your guidance in this awesome new responsibility. May our leaders never forget their duty to the people they lead, and to their families who love them. May they instill in those under their command the qualities of loyalty, integrity, and duty. Grant them patience in dealing with the mistakes of others. Let them remember that for fragile humans, perfection means trying each day to be better than the day before.

Give them courage, O Lord, in the face of danger. Keep them pure in heart, clear in mind, and strong in purpose. Remind them that wisdom is not found in an hour, a day, or a year, but that gaining it is a process that continues throughout our lives. Keep our goal not to perpetuate war but to safeguard peace ever before us, and preserve your great gift of freedom.

May you always be near to guide them in their decisions, comfort them in their failures, and keep them humble in their success. We ask for your divine blessing for them. Inspire their leadership as they discharge the honor and responsibility of leading soldiers and civilians in the service of their country. We thank you for this day, and for the knowledge that you are with us in and through all things.

In your holy name, we pray.
Amen.

> Chaplain Lt. Col. Mark E. Thompson
> Deputy/Senior Clinician
> EAMC DMPC

LEADERSHIP

Most gracious Lord,
Hear this prayer from your humble servant.
You create and you sustain. You are indeed holy
love. May your hopes for mankind be realized,
even in those places where hatred seems to run
rampant. May all of us who wear the uniform
honor you as well as the country we serve.
Keep us free from retaliating in anger, but
strong enough to defend those liberties that we
cherish. Soften the hearts of those who wish to
do us harm. Impart wisdom to our leadership
of all ranks. Watch over our families when
we are separated from them. May they always
know of our love for them.

Do not let my needs take precedence over the
needs of those service members in my charge.
You have kept me alive thus far, and I am
grateful to you. You have given me Christian
brothers and sisters to serve beside me.

You have calmed my heart when danger
loomed so close. May my life, from this day
forward, be a testament to you. One day,
you will be pleased with all of your creation.
Until then, may you be pleased with my efforts.
Forgive my many failings, and pour out your
grace upon all of us who desire to live better
in every way. I offer my heart even now to you,
because of your great expression of love,
in the form of your Son, Jesus.
Amen.

Chaplain Col. Dennis M. Goodwin
United States Army Reserve

INSPIRATION AND COURAGE

Lord our God,
In our world of competing faiths, conflicting
theories, and antagonistic politics, we become
confused in our search for truth, and
sometimes just stop searching.

There seem to be more gray areas than
absolutes of right and wrong. Answers raise
additional questions. We question ideas that
we were once sure about. Some of the teachings
our parents gave us have been discredited.
Some really good people hold convictions
different from our own, and some folks
with impeccable spiritual credentials have
disillusioned us with their lives. Overall,
we're less sure of things than we once were.

So, we come to you humbly, acknowledging our role as seekers. We're not disheartened, for we know that you walk with us. We're not discouraged, for we find excitement and satisfaction in the journey. We don't despair, because we know that you accept us even in our weakness.

Creator and sustainer God, you loved the world so much that you gave your son. Help us to follow in his footsteps in working to create a better world. Help us as we promote new levels of justice and equality in our land. Help us as we conserve the rich traditions of the past without being immobilized by them.

Help us to seek the healing of sick people, rehabilitation of prisoners, and freedom for those who suffer from addictions. Open our eyes to the needs of the people who sit in the cubicle next to us, live in the room next door, and who sit next to us in church.

In a world of anger and animosity, help us to make peace. Allow us to seek to advance those people who are less privileged, and to educate those people who seem to lack opportunity.

Help us to set a personal example that will inspire and encourage others so that they may, in turn, inspire and encourage others.

Hear us, now, as we pray together as your Son has taught us:

Our Father...

Amen.

Chaplain Lt. Col. Mark E. Thompson
Deputy/Senior Clinician
EAMC DMPC

BRIGADE BLESSING

Lord our God,
The human face can communicate so many
things.

In our world, we see faces of peace and faces of
war; faces of death and faces of want; faces of
joy and faces of sadness.

In times past, when the faces of courage and
sacrifice were needed, we were blessed with
men and women who offered their lives, and did
not doubt that it was right.

Today, we remember those who have gone
before us. We pray for those people who are in
harm's way right now, and we ask your blessing
on this brigade as we prepare ourselves to
answer our nation's call.

In your name, we pray.
Amen.

Chaplain Lt. Col. Mark E. Thompson
Deputy/Senior Clinician
EAMC DMPC

PHYSICAL AND MENTAL FATIGUE

God,

We have so many demands put upon us every day, particularly as families dealing with the challenges of deployment and separations. Help me, God, to understand that while circumstances can drain our resources and leave us depleted, you are always there for us. You've promised that life will not leave us as empty vessels or dry up our spirits. As we face these demands each day, remind us of our inner resources and strength. Greater are you within us than anyone who is outside of us.

We can become physically and mentally drained, but we pray to you, O God, to supply us with divine strength. Our economy can become warped, but your richness and glory will move us beyond that. Something positive can come from negative situations. We can come from mental fatigue to mental strength.

We can come from emotional strain to emotional strength. God, help us to place positive thoughts into the midst of negative messages that cripple our spirit. God, since you are the great supplier, we will come to you for our needs. We thank you, God, for placing people on this earth who can and will pray for us. You told us in the Scriptures that if we pray for one another, you will heal us. (See James 5:16.) God, there is a saying that helps me during the day: "Little prayer, little power; no prayer, no power; but a lot of prayer, a lot of power." This power comes from you, God, and I need it every day to get by for myself and for those around me.

Amen.

Chaplain Lt. Col. Ted Whitely
Air National Guard

RIGHTEOUSNESS

Ah, you who are wise in your own eyes,
and shrewd in your own sight!

Isaiah 5:21

Reflection

We all like to think of ourselves as wise and
reliable in judgment. This perception is an
obstacle to truth. I have to accept the truth
about the desperate condition of my heart,
soul, and mind. Acceptance is a radical step
and act of my will. If I do not make this step,
the deception will hinder my ability to perform
the duties that my rank requires. Anyone who
ever speaks of faith as an easy answer to life's
hardness knows nothing of it. Repentance
and regeneration are radical terms suggesting
radical changes. Jesus described this in terms
of tearing out an eye, or cutting off a hand.
(See Mark 9:43-47.) The truth is that I am not

wise; my judgment is not reliable without a radical change, involving personal repentance and God's sanctifying grace that makes me a new creation. This process continues until my death.

Prayer

Father, remove all conceit and vestiges of pride from my heart, mind, and soul. Forgive me, renew me, and make me whole and righteous in your sight for Jesus' sake.
Amen.

Chaplain Col. Kenneth N. Brown
Multi-National Corps-Iraq

LOOK AFTER MY FAMILY

Our faith guides us through many challenges and tests in our lives, none of them greater than separation from loved ones. Whether it's the first time we head out the door to Basic Military Training, our first duty station, a short temporary-duty assignment, a remote tour, or a war in a foreign land, separation is never easy.

I have experienced all of these scenarios. I have left my wife and small children many times over my career. It seemed that every time I would depart, a challenge would present itself: the car would break down, a child would get sick, a bill needed to be paid—you name it. I, like many members of the military, was blessed to share my life with a very strong partner, my wife Mary. No matter the challenge, she always said, "Well, we have this problem or that challenge, but don't worry about it. I will take care of it!" And she always did, without question. She made it possible for me to go to college; she basically raised our kids because I was always on the road, and she did a simply wonderful job. I will never forget the many temporary-duty assignments where I had to leave the family for a period of time. None of them were easy, but none were as difficult as the day in 2003 when I departed my house for a duty assignment taking me to one of the most dangerous places in Afghanistan. Sure, I was confident in my training and experience to be successful in my duties, but knowing it was a true "combat zone" made me a bit more apprehensive. But I couldn't let my wife and kids see the fear running through my mind about how challenging it would be. I prayed every night to return home safely, and not to show my concern to my family. The day I departed was like any other, or so I thought. As I completed my packing, I was never alone. Either my wife or one of the kids was there with me and never left my side. As I grabbed my bags and headed out the door, I looked back to see our three young children standing on the balcony of our home, crying. It was then I realized that it was more difficult for them than it was for me. But as I climbed into the car, my wife said, "Don't worry; I have it all under control!" And, as usual, she did. As I boarded the aircraft for Afghanistan, I prayed, not for me, but for them! After all, I realized that the only reason I was able to serve my country in a time of war was because of the support I received from my wife and children. Now I am the "guy on the balcony" as I watch our son head off to his deployments, as he has chosen to serve his country and follow in my footsteps. It's now my turn to pray for his safe return and let him know that "I have it under control!"

Chief Master Sgt. (Ret.) Kenneth J. McQuiston

MISSING FAMILY

Almighty God,
I've been feeling down and out because I miss my family so much. You've blessed me with a wonderful family who loves and supports me in this mission to serve my country. Now, as I find myself separated from them by many miles, their welfare weighs heavily on my soul.

Dear God, bless them every day. Keep them safe in your arms and free from harm. As they go about their lives back home, remind them of my great love for them and your love for them as well.

O God, the memory of my family runs deep in my spirit. Thank you for those good memories of my family members, both living and deceased.

O God, if I don't return home to them, may they know that their faces were on my mind and in my heart to the very end.

Abide with them until I see them back home or
am reunited with them in heaven.

Hear my plea, O Lord.
Amen.

Chaplain Lt. Col. David I. Lee
Alabama Army National Guard
226th Area Support Group

VICTORY

Almighty God,
You reign on high, raise the downtrodden,
and bring down the mighty empires. Bless
us today, and grant the continued success of
our missions. Spread your wings of protection
upon our soldiers far from home, and upon
their family members back at home. Send your
wisdom to the president of the United States of
America and our commanders, so that we are
victorious over our enemies and able to have
everlasting peace at home.
Amen.

Chaplain Andrew Shulman
94th Military Police Battalion
USAG Yongsan Seoul, Korea

NEW ASSIGNMENT

Dear Lord,
Here we are again
in a new assignment:
a new home, new schools,
new friends, and new challenges.

Lord, you know that we are proud
　　to serve this nation
And to defend it, each in our own way:
In the field, supporting our soldiers,
And in the home, supporting our soldier.
You support us in this mission,
And help us to keep your most holy mission
　　alive in our hearts.

Help me, Lord, to make this transition
　　smooth for my family.
Give me the grace to see the adventure
　　over the adversity;
the patience to deal with boxes in the hall
　　and changes in the routine;

the organization to keep track of changing
	expectations and new requirements;
the wisdom to know what to say to strangers
	I meet and to my own children
	as they adjust;
the strength to deal with unplanned surprises
	and unexpected tears;
and the vision to recognize opportunities
	and new joys.

Lord, you brought us to this life.
Stand by us in this tour;
walk with us through this time;
guide us gently to the wonderful things here.
And, when time comes to pack the car
	and move on,
hold us close and protect us on our next move.
Amen.

Capt. Karina Fabian
United States Air Force, Separated
Wife of Col. Robert Fabian
United States Air Force

AMBITION

Likewise, just as it was in the days of Lot:
they were eating and drinking, buying and selling,
planting and building, but on the day that
Lot left Sodom, it rained fire and sulfur
from heaven and destroyed all of them….

Luke 17:28–29

Reflection

What's wrong with buying, selling, planting,
and building? There is nothing wrong unless
the activity is the sole focus of a person's life.
In Lot's day they thought about nothing but
themselves. This "me focus" so absorbed their
lives that they made no time for God. This
displeased God and resulted in devastating
judgment. God wants us to see worldly affairs
from the perspective of our relationship to him.
We're not expected to renounce all interest
in the affairs of this life, but to keep them
subordinate to the Lord at all times. That's true
even of times of deployment and separation.
It is so easy to become obsessed with the

things and people and worries around us that we forget about God and the fact that he is the Supreme Being. When he is our priority, we find that our daily living is lifted up and inspired by him. Without him, we become invested in the "city of Sodom perspective" and divested of the city of God.

Prayer

Heavenly Father, it's so easy to become absorbed in earthly ambition and concerns. May my family back home and I wear this world as a loose garment to be tossed away without a second thought.
Amen.

Chaplain Col. Kenneth N. Brown
Multi-National Corps-Iraq (MNC-I) Command Chaplain

SOLDIER'S PRAYER

When bullets fly and bombs blow,
upon our knees, dear Lord, we go.
We pray for safety, pray for strength,
for inner peace for the length
of time away from ones at home,
who love us still where e'er we roam.
Dear God, my arms are not that long
to reach out to them, to keep them strong.
But your arms are long and stronger still.
Keep them safe within thy will.
Bring them comfort, bring them peace,
until from duty I'm released.
Back to those whom I love best.
We thank you, Lord, to have passed this test.
Amen.

Chaplain Maj. James R. Lewis
Ohio Army National Guard

FOR MY DEAR WIFE

Lord, my heart breaks for the love of my life;
so loyal and patient is my loving wife.

Lord, she's such a gift, none else can compare
with the blessing she is,
    yet now I've left her there.
Lord, grant her your strength,
    though she's ever so strong.
Keep her in your care,
    though I'm gone far too long.
Give her your wisdom for our little ones;
    let her be the model for daughters and sons.
Give her patience to spare when
    the going gets rough.
For Lord, how I know, going solo is tough.
Let her tears fertilize our love while I'm away.
Somehow, let her know how I love her today.
Keep her growing strong in her trust
    that's in you.
Help her know, for her cares,
    that's the best thing to do.
Into your strong hands, I entrust my dear wife.
Let her never forget, she's the love of my life.
Amen.

Chaplain Maj. James R. Lewis
Ohio Army National Guard

FOR A SOLDIER'S SON

God, bless my dear son while I am,
  from him, away.
Let him know that I love him,
  always and today.
Inspire his small soul with a Godly
  man's dreams,
to what is right, not for what pleasure seems.
In the midst of his fears,
  let him your courage know,
so he's strong and courageous,
  when to danger I go.

Help him to be good for his mom, to support,
whether playing with a sibling or
  playing at sport.
Remind him to fall to his small knees in prayer
when he's restless with fear
  or distracted with care.
Help him take pride in his duties and chores,
while I'm far and away on distant land's shores.
Hold him to your heart in your strong
  loving arm,

till I'm safe by his side and no more near
    war's harm.
Amen.

Chaplain Maj. James R. Lewis
Ohio Army National Guard

A PRAYER FOR THOSE ASHORE

Loving Lord,
You did not remain on high,
but came and walked among us.
You promised not to abandon us or
    to leave us as orphans.
We turn to you, O Lord, to do what we cannot.
Please be present to those we left on shore.
Comfort them in our absence,
protect them as we sail,
and prepare us all for our reunion
    when the voyage is over.
We pray in the name of the Father, and the Son,
and the Holy Spirit.
Amen.

Chaplain Lt. Jason M. Constantine
United States Naval Reserves

TRIUMPH OF JUSTICE

We bless you, O Lord of heaven and earth, for your goodness and gentle power. You rule your creation with such firmness that we stand in awe of your great majesty. Yet you treat us, your creatures, with such respect that we can only marvel at your great patience.

We praise you for your mighty power. It renews our confidence in the triumph of justice. Yet we rejoice at the restraint with which you use your power. It restores our hope for forgiveness.

Dear God, we wish we didn't have to ask for your forgiveness, but only for your justice. Yet we could never survive your just judgment of us. We have sinned with our minds, entertaining thoughts that serve no good purpose. We have sinned with our hands, doing things we hope no one will ever know. We have sinned with our lips, saying things that never should have been said. We have sinned with our hearts, not loving you with all our being, not loving our neighbor as ourselves.

For all our sins, O God, we ask your forgiveness. Remove them from us as far as the east is from the west (see Psalm 103:12), and renew in us such an awareness of your presence that we can no more let go of you than you can let go of us.

The world in which you have placed us is full of trouble and challenge. Grant us the ability to see its possibilities and the courage to make them happen. Where there is despair, let us bring hope; where there is oppression let us bring justice; where there is doubt, let us awaken faith; where there is violence, let us wage peace.

Help us, O God, in this world torn by strife and bitterness, to experience and spread the joy of seeing your will done on earth and heaven. We thank you for all our many blessings, and ask you to ensure safety for those who are not able to be with us this day. Bring them and us safely home again, and hear us now as we pray together.
Amen.

Chaplain Lt. Col. Mark E. Thompson
Deputy/Senior Clinician
EAMC DMPC

THE ROAD OF LIFE

(A prayer-poem written for a little boy in the Midwest who was born a couple of days after his father was killed in Iraq)

You may not remember me;
I met you on the road.
You were in a hurry
and I held a heavy load.

What's that thing? you asked me.
It's a tool to keep you free,
so someday we can live in peace,
and you can grow up just like me.

Where is it you're going?
I'm headed for that light.
A pretty lady waits there,
and she'll watch you day and night.

Wouldn't you like to join me?
It sounds like lots of fun.
No, I'm here to see you off
before my time is done.

Nice to have met you.
The pleasure was all mine.
I'm afraid that I didn't get your name.
Actually, you did! But "Dad" will do just fine.

Capt. Robert Longley
United States Air Force

THANKSGIVING DAY

God,
As we pause to acknowledge your presence,
we know that gratitude sets in motion a
chain reaction that transforms all around us,
including ourselves.

We thank you for your transforming love, and
we pray that your love in us, and for us, might
flow into the lives of those around us.

We ask for your continued blessings upon
those who gather here, and their families and
friends so far away. We are especially thankful
for those who cannot be with us, those who
have made the greatest sacrifice of all, giving
their lives so that we might enjoy our freedom
on this Thanksgiving Day.

We thank you for this food; we ask for your
blessing upon it, and upon those who have
made this day so special for us.

We ask this in your blessed name. Amen.

Chaplain Lt. Col. Mark E. Thompson
Deputy/Senior Clinician
EAMC DMPC

A CHRISTMAS PRAYER

Our heavenly Father,
May Christmas penetrate our deepest souls
until we experience the true light that shone
at Bethlehem. May that light shine brightly
from within us until all the darkness from fear,
ignorance, and prejudice is dispelled, and all of
the world's people are free to live out the noble
creed of brotherliness and true equality.

Finally, Father, we pray that the entire
community may know the joy and peace that
this holy season proclaims, and receive your
rich blessings throughout the New Year.

For the glory of your name, we pray.
Amen.

Chaplain Col. Henry L. Hunt
HQ, FORSCOM

CHRISTMAS AND NEW YEAR'S

Loving Father,
Help us remember the birth of Jesus,
so that we may share in the song of the angels,
the gladness of the shepherds, and the worship
of the wise men.

Close the door of hate, and open the door of
love all over the world. Let kindness come
with every gift, and good desires with every
greeting. Deliver us from evil by the blessing
that Christ brings, and teach us to be merry
with clear hearts.

May each day of this New Year be like
Christmas morning, making us happy to be
your children. May each evening bring us to
our beds with grateful thoughts, forgiving and
forgiven, for Jesus' sake.
Amen.

Chaplain Lt. Col. Mark E. Thompson
Deputy/Senior Clinician
EAMC DMPC

PRAYER FOR
ABSENT FAMILY MEMBERS

O God, whose fatherly care reaches to the
uttermost parts of the earth; We humbly
beseech you graciously to behold and bless
those whom we love, now absent from us.
Defend them from all dangers of soul and body,
and grant that both they and we, drawing
nearer to you, may be bound together by your
love in the communion of your Holy Spirit;
through Jesus Christ our Lord.
Amen.

Anonymous

COMRADES IN ARMS, BROTHERS AND SISTERS IN OUR HEARTS...

Many would think that one of the greatest experiences of serving our nation is the opportunity to travel around the world. And yes, it is a significant advantage over many other occupations. I have lived in Texas, New Jersey, Delaware, Mississippi, and Illinois (twice), and have lived abroad in Turkey, Germany, and Afghanistan. I have also been blessed to travel to almost every other country, with the exception of China and Russia. But through it all, it wasn't the locations I visited that were so important—it was the people I met along the way.

Regardless of which service a person belongs to, one of the greatest things about serving in the military is sharing time with people who have incredibly diverse backgrounds. It is possible to learn so much from every person one comes in contact with. Sure, individuals will meet some service members they may not be too fond of, but they definitely can learn from everyone. No matter their home, their financial situation, their educational background, the color of their skin, or even the faith they believe in, people usually have more in common than they might think. The one "constant" is that all of us chose to serve, and to serve something that is much bigger than we are as individuals. And regardless of how long we serve in the armed forces, and where our paths in life take us, we will always have that bond. No matter where we wind up, we will always know that there will be a warm bed, hot meal, and a cool drink if we need it. We are a band of brothers and sisters who have shared some of the most incredible highs and, for some, the greatest of challenges along the way. This bond transcends the branch of the armed forces one serves in, or even the country served. I have been blessed to work with members of all branches of the U.S. Armed Forces. I've also worked with service members of other nations; they, like us, have chosen a life of service, a life that will forever keep us bound together like a family—it's a great feeling!

Chief Master Sgt. (Ret.) Kenneth J. McQuiston

A SOLDIER'S PRAYER

Lord Jesus, Mighty Warrior and Prince of
Peace, all glory and power is yours, I offer
myself and my military career for the welfare
of our nation and for your glory.

You said "Blessed is the nation whose God is
the Lord"; make us mindful of our nation's
heritage and of who we are. You said, "Be
strong and of good courage." This is my prayer.
You said, "A King is not saved by his great
army; a warrior is not delivered by his great
strength"; be my protection and my strength.
While I defend the nation, may all of heaven
safeguard my family back home.

Almighty God, when you will to safely return
me home, help me to see in each member of my
family all that I am willing to fight for—life,
liberty, freedom, and justice. Give me wisdom
to share what experiences would lead my
sons to Christ—like valor, my daughters to
Christian compassion. When Mary witnessed
you falling wounded to the ground, she

reaffirmed her trust in God her savior. Fill my
spouse with surety in your divine plan for me,
our family and our nation. You called me to be
a soldier, march along side me. Jesus, I place
my trust in you.
Amen.

Anonymous

THE UNEXPECTED

Lord God, there are times I feel so alone and
ill prepared when faced with the unknown.
I try to be prepared for the unexpected, but I
need your help. In these times, walk with me,
place your hand on my shoulder, and guide my
footsteps. Make me aware that I am in your
company, and am surrounded by a great crowd
of heavenly witnesses.

In Christ's name, I pray.
Amen.

Chaplain Capt. David R. Vaughn
United States Civil Air Patrol
Group 1 Headquarters, Chaplain
Tennessee Wing

DEATH OF A SOLDIER

Almighty God,
Our hearts are saddened by the loss of all
those who have given their lives to sustain the
freedom that we so richly enjoy. Bring your
comforting Spirit to the families and friends
of these courageous men and women.
Grant, O God, your peace and love to all of
them, for you alone can fill their emptiness
with hope. We entrust them to your care.

Help us to draw creatively upon the limitless
resources that you've provided. May we be
brave so that the enemy won't succeed in
depriving us of our freedom.

Grant us wisdom to solve problems and enrich
life. Fill us with compassion for those in
need, inspire us to live by your word, cease
oppression, help freedom prevail, and assure
that dignity and honor reign. Then we shall
know that the hero we honor today will not
have died in vain.

We offer our prayer in your holy name.
Amen.

Chaplain Lt. Col. Mark E. Thompson
Deputy/Senior Clinician
EAMC DMPC

ASKING DIVINE PROTECTION
FOR THOSE IN SERVICE

O God, I beseech you, watch over those
exposed to the horror of war, and the spiritual
dangers of a soldier or sailor's life.

Give them such a strong faith that no human
respect may ever lead them to deny it, nor fear
ever to practice it. By your grace, O God, fortify
them against the contagion of bad example,
that being preserved from vice, and serving you
faithfully, they may be ready to meet you face
to face when they are so called, through Christ
our Lord.
Amen.

Anonymous

GRIEF

Almighty God,
Please help us in our darkest hour of grief. Help us to remember that you are in control. Help us to hang on to you when we feel like giving in to despair, knowing that you will give us the strength not to lose heart. Thank you for these men and women, for their dedication to duty, for their courage and loyalty, for their faith in you. Thank you for bringing them into your presence to be with you forever. Help us to hang on to that hope of life eternal, to walk by faith and not by sight, to have the courage your Scripture speaks of, and to please you as we encourage one another. Please hold close the families of these soldiers.

In your holy and loving name, we pray.
Amen.

Chaplain Col. Kerry Haynes
United States Army Reserves

HONORING OUR HEROES

Almighty and awesome God,
You stand shoulder to shoulder on this field
of America's heroes, each one a volunteer and
patriot of our great nation, each one trained to
support and defend the values they hold dear.

Father, as strong as we are, we recognize that
there is one greater than us, and ask your
blessing as we go off to war. This is nothing
new for you, God. You went before Gideon
and Joshua, Moses and David, and you have
gone before many American battles, past and
present. So we humbly ask that you go before
this brigade with your blessing as a shield and
sword. Lead us and guide us, God. Protect us,
and protect and comfort our family members
who will anxiously await our return. Give us all
the courage of a lion as we face the unknown—
and the vision of an eagle to see the victory in
our future. In your holy name, we pray. Amen.

Chaplain Maj. James Foster
United States Army

FALLEN COMRADES

Gracious God and Loving Father,
We just received the news we never wanted
to hear concerning the death of our beloved
comrades. For so long, they have been our
brothers and sisters in the line of duty and
service. We have grown together through
mutual faith, and now our hearts have become
heavy in that they have given the ultimate
sacrifice for our country. We were friends;
we were family; we were comrades; we were
brothers and sisters; and now they are no more.
Receive them, O Lord, into your kingdom. We
had hoped for a safe return for all, but now we
return without some who were our very best.

As you comfort their loved ones, comfort us as well. Thank you for the privilege of serving beside our fallen patriots. Grant us hope, grant us peace, grant us strength, and grant us courage for facing the days ahead. Help us know that in the midst of life and death, you are always with us. Thank you, Lord.
Amen.

Chaplain Lt. Col. David I. Lee
Alabama Army National Guard
226th Area Support Group
Operation Iraqi Freedom
Camp Arifjan, Kuwait

LIVING AS BEST AS I CAN

My dearest Lord,
There is so much to pray for, and so much to
ask forgiveness for these days. I offer to you the
countless family members and others for whom
I pray. I believe you know their needs, and
will answer their concerns, even if I don't list
them by name. Lord, I'm a simple sinner who
tries to do the best I can under these difficult
circumstances of working, making decisions,
and living. I live as best as I can with the
pressures of debt, personal issues, and other
weighty matters that seem impossible for me.
But in my heart of hearts, I know you can make
all the difference in any outcome I lay before
you. Lord, always and in whatever way you see
fit, give me the grace, as I wear this uniform,
to be a person of good character who is
merciful towards others and kind to myself.

Help me to accept the responsibilities given to me. It isn't easy living these days in or out of this uniform. But Lord, let your will be done, not mine. Let me know that I am loved and can love others; forgive and not hate; be one noted for integrity and doing right, when others seem to follow what is the easy road. Lord, I ask simply that you carry me, take me as I am, and give me strength to walk with others.

I pray in your gracious name,
Amen.

Chaplain Gary Stickney
United States Army

FAITHFULNESS

Let us hold fast to the confession of our hope
without wavering, for he who has promised
is faithful.

Hebrews 10:23

Reflection

On a recent trip, I heard a young chaplain share
the following questions: "I am on my third
Iraq deployment. I have personally conducted
twenty-eight memorial ceremonies. How many
more must I do? How many more times must I
come back? How do I keep doing this?" I had
encouraged frank, open questions, and this one
was the hardest I had ever received. The answer
I gave went something like this: "I understand
the heart-wrenching pain you are experiencing.
I am, too, and so are many others. The reason
I know this is because you are another human
being just like me, with the same kinds of
sorrow, doubt, fear, frustration, joy, and
sadness. I don't know how long, or how many
more, but this one thing I do know for sure.

However many times we come back; however many memorial ceremonies we conduct; all of it is based on the promise we made. At the end of this war, come what may politically, or institutionally as an Army, the survival of both are balanced on that promise. This is not changed, nor will it ever change. The only change that can turn the course of a nation is for even a few to go back on their solemn promise."

Prayer

O Lord, strengthen me that I may be faithful to the promise I have made, knowing that you are always faithful to keep yours.
Amen.

Chaplain Col. Kenneth N. Brown
Multi-National Corps-Iraq (MNC-I) Command Chaplain

MOVING FORWARD

Gather up my spirit,
and raise my fallen flag.
Call for reinforcements
before you put me in a bag.

I am but a vessel,
the tip of freedom's spear.
Call another forward
to help rid the world of fear.

Take my essence with you
as you move on towards your goal.
Remember what we fight for,
and don't worry about the toll.

Remember me in victory,
for it is triumph that I've seen.
In life or death you'll know me
as a proud U.S. Marine.

Capt. Robert Longley

BATTLE PRAYER

Into battle now we fly, though sometimes,
Lord, we wonder why.
If peace on earth is still our call,
why go to battle where some will fall?
But for our families, for our land,
we take these weapons now in hand.
Let right prevail and win the day;
keep us safe, dear Lord, we pray.
Let leaders quickly make the choice
that liberty may have a voice.
Let battle's end decide the day,
that peace again may reign, we pray.
Amen.

Chaplain Maj. James Lewis
Ohio Army National Guard

WHEN BATTLE RAGES
INTO THE NIGHT

Into the valley of death we go,
as shadows fall all around.
We fear the darkness hides our foe,
as we seek safety's ground.
Keep eyes and minds alert, we pray,
within our boundary laid.
Confuse their minds, confound their paths,
please keep our foe's hand stayed.
When bullets fly and bombs blast,
keep us strong, Lord, hold us fast.
Help us withstand whatever they throw,
until the dark of night does go.
When morning's light then brings its cheer,
let it banish every fear.
Into thy hands we trust our care, Lord,
let your courage fill the night air.
Give us strength to last the night, Lord,
into your hands we place this fight.
Amen.

Chaplain Maj. James Lewis
Ohio Army National Guard

Intercession for Those at Sea

For all those who rely on the sea,
let us pray to the Lord.
Lord, have mercy.

For the protection of the ships,
let us pray to the Lord.
Christ, have mercy.

That the officers may be granted wisdom,
let us pray to the Lord.
Lord, have mercy.

That the crews may have courage
in the tempest,
let us pray to the Lord.
Christ, have mercy.

That we may be comforted in their absence,
let us pray to the Lord.
Lord, have mercy.

That the Lord may be present to all those
still on patrol,
let us pray to the Lord.
Christ, have mercy.

Let us remember that we are not alone.
Christ said that the Holy Spirit is with us all,
whether at sea or on shore. And so, when we
gather to worship, we do so together, regardless
of our physical location or placement in time.
Amen.

Chaplain Lt. Jason M. Constantine
United States Naval Reserves

A PRAYER FOR THOSE AT SEA

Eternal Father,
Your Spirit swept across the waters, bringing
order to chaos, and you brought forth land that
binds the mighty deep to its limits. Your Son,
our Lord, commanded the waves to be still, and
they obeyed him. May you protect those who
are on the waters and in the waves. Grant them
fair winds and following seas that they may
return safely to us on shore.

For all of this, we pray in the name of Christ
Jesus our Lord.
Amen.

Chaplain Lt. Jason M. Constantine
United States Naval Reserves

SACRIFICES

Lord our God,
You ordered this wondrous world, and know all things in earth and heaven. Let us always remember the sacrifices of those men and women who have gone before us, and of those who, at this very moment, find themselves in harm's way, defending this nation that we so love. As we come together this evening, fill our hearts with renewed trust in you, that by night and day in all seasons, we may bravely commit all that we have and hope to be. We thank you for all you have given us and for the fellowship of good friends.

In your holy name, we pray.
Amen.

Chaplain Lt. Col. Mark E. Thompson
Deputy/Senior Clinician
EAMC DMPC

FOREVER A SERVICEMEMBER...

I am truly a blessed man! After twenty-eight years in uniform—twenty-four of them married to the woman of my dreams—I have traveled the world and served as a part of the "institution of freedom." As I transition to the next stage of life, I look forward with great excitement and anticipate new opportunities. I know there will be some big challenges for me and my family along the way; after all, I have lived the military lifestyle for my entire adult life and then it all changes in the blink of an eye. A friend who retired a few years ago told me, "You go from flying mach two, to riding your bicycle through a school zone." And that prediction has proven true. My role now will be to "cheer from the sidelines" for those who will replace me and continue the fight for freedom; I will be there for them, as many have been for me.

For me, there are some very positive aspects to moving into the "next phase of life." First is the blessing that comes from having had the opportunity to contribute to the defense of our nation, and the knowledge that my efforts have had a positive effect on many people across the globe. Second, I have had the opportunity to make more friends around the world than a person should be able to in a lifetime. Third, I have also become a better husband and father from the learning experiences I have had along the way, and hopefully I will be able to share those experiences with others. But lastly, I have a better relationship with God. Because on the day I stepped out the door and headed for Basic Military Training, I started to pray; I haven't stopped yet. I know that there isn't a challenge in my life that I can't overcome as long as I have my family by my side and God in my heart.

Chief Master Sgt. (Ret.) Kenneth J. McQuiston

DEMONS OF WAR

Dear God,
I pray for all those who are serving or have
served our country. I pray that they will know
that they have brother and sister veterans
who they can call on in time of need. Please
don't ever let them get down on themselves
and decide that life isn't worth living. Assure
them, Lord that they can deal with the demons
they may have brought back from war. Please
help them to be all that they can be and give
them courage to call a friend or fellow veteran
when the going gets tough. Please give them
the strength to ask for help when they need
it. Lord, they have fought and served our
country, and this nation owes them gratitude
and thanks. Boot camp is tough, going to war
is tougher, and coming home is the greatest
challenge of all. Be with them, Lord, as they
proceed through each of these stages in their
lives. Bless and keep them safe now and always.
Amen.

Jeff "Doc" Dentice
United States Army E-5 Medic
Vietnam

CONTINUING THE JOURNEY

Even the sparrow finds a home,
and the swallow a nest for herself,
where she may lay her young,
at your altars, O LORD of hosts,
my King and my God.

Psalm 84:3

Reflection

Every non-rational creature instinctively seeks its home near the altar of God. A human being, on the other hand, has a will and can draw near to God or not. He's prepared a place for us in his temple. (See Revelation 3:12.) Jesus says, "...I go to prepare a place for you [us]" (John 14:2). Our place is prepared and awaits us. It was prepared before we were even created—prior to the foundations of the world. The only way we will not arrive at our place is to reject God's love. Then and only then our name will be blotted out from the Lamb's book of life. (See Revelation 13:8.)

Prayer

God of glory, as I continue my journey on this earth in and out of military service, may I hunger and thirst for you until I arrive at my place near your altar.
Amen.

Chaplain Col. Kenneth N. Brown
Multi-National Corps-Iraq (MNC-I) Command Chaplain

ALONG BESIDE THEM

Dear Lord,
Although I've hung up my boots and my BDUs, I still have many military friends that need you. It's hard not to be in a squadron out there, knowing that I should be fighting right along beside them. My commitment with Uncle Sam might have come to an end, but the love for my military family will never fade. Keep them safe, give them strength, and bring all of my friends home soon.
Amen.

Senior Airman Rhina Portillochacon
375th Airlift Wing Public Affairs, Separated

STONE MEMORIES

Their sacrifice is lined in rows,
side by side, and head to toe.
Some have crosses, others stars;
some wore stripes, others bars.

A generation lost to God,
for whom a nation cried;
a memory now almost lost
of how and why they died.

Perhaps it's just the way of things,
and in wars throughout all time,
that nations give their finest,
to be cut down in their prime.

Or maybe it's the price of peace,
and the hope of lessons learned.
If so, then don't forget them,
or the thanks that they have earned.

Capt. Robert Longley
United States Air Force

THE UNIFORM

It's not just in the uniform
that everyone can see.
It's more in the simple dream
of what America should be.

Where people sleep in comfort,
without the thought of fear,
because someone in uniform
stands ready, poised and near,

to defend the Constitution,
and preserve our way of life,
standing watch in times of peace
and ready for times of strife.

You may not see them every day,
those of honor, in green and blue.
But they are there to fight and die,
to preserve the dream for you.

Capt. Robert Longley
United States Air Force

PATRIOT DAY

Gracious and ever-present source of our being
and hope, we pause to remember the lives of
those who were suddenly and tragically taken
from us in wanton acts of senseless violence.
We humbly remember, and pay our last respects
for the incredibly noble and heroic sacrifices
made by those who were there providing first-
line protection, service, and defense on that
fateful morning—September 11, 2001. Quicken
our thoughts and help us to rightly recall the
lives of all who perished, so that we can affirm
our commitment to the ideas and ideals that
continue to unite Americans in the aftermath of
those terrible deeds. May we focus this day not
on the devastation, but rather, O God, help us
to focus on the patriotism, valor, and incredible
honor shown by those who gave their last full
measure of devotion.

We ask this in your most holy and precious name.
Amen.

Chaplain Lt. Col. Steven R. George
42nd Military Police/BDE Command Chaplain
Fort Lewis, WA

FOR OUR MILITARY AT CHRISTMAS

Almighty God and heavenly Father,
We come together to worship and honor you,
gathered from many places to celebrate the
birth of our Lord and Savior, Jesus Christ. As
we assemble here, we remember those of us
who are in active service to our country. While
we are here, our fellow soldiers are in faraway
places and approaching this holy season in
a completely different setting. Many of them
are living in tents or sleeping on the cold, wet
ground. Comfort them where they are as you
comfort us wherever we are. We pray for them
tonight, men and women who have made many
sacrifices for our country and for us. Bless them
and keep them safe and close to you. Bless our
country and our world with peace.
Amen.

Chaplain Lt. Col. David I. Lee
Alabama Army National Guard
226th Area Support Group
Operation Iraqi Freedom
Camp Arifjan, Kuwait

RETIREMENT

Almighty God,
Please bless our retired soldiers. Remind us how quickly time passes, and how important it is to live well and serve faithfully. Let us honor them, let us commemorate how they have honored us through their service.

Lord, we thank you for the soldiers who have served so faithfully, for their dedication and their sacrifice to our country. We are equally thankful for the sacrifices made by their families. Place your arms of protection around them. Guide them in their transition to civilian life, supply them with patience, and bless them with prosperity. Continue to grant them wisdom, vision, and courage as they strive to build your kingdom with you here on earth. Amen.

Chaplain Lt. Col. Mark E. Thompson
Deputy/Senior Clinician
EAMC DMPC

INACTIVATION

Almighty God,
We thank you for those who have gone before
us to make this day possible, and especially for
those who have given the ultimate sacrifice for
our freedom.

Lord our God, you have filled our lives with
many changes and challenging opportunities.
You've given each of us the capacity to enjoy
the wonders of this world. You have enabled us
to dream and to be inspired. Awaken us, Lord,
to the promise of this new day. Add meaning
to our lives, so that our minds may grow in
knowledge and wisdom, and bless us with your
loving presence as we go from this place.

In your name we pray.
Amen.

> Chaplain Lt. Col. Mark E. Thompson
> Deputy/Senior Clinician
> EAMC DMPC

TOMORROW

…and in front of the throne there is something like a sea of glass, like crystal.

Revelation 4:6

Reflection

As a small boy, I loved to draw, especially airplanes, even though they never appeared on paper the way they appeared in my mind. It's hard to portray three-dimensional objects on a one-dimensional surface. It's the same with some of the thoughts I have about the mysteries of God. It's a lot like drawing those airplanes years ago. Perhaps we're all constrained in that regard, but that shouldn't prevent us from seeking to know and understand God.

Prayer

Lord of glory, I'll never know all of your mysteries, nor all that you have planned for me in the ages to come. Nor can I fully understand all of the experiences and impressions that are

part of my military service. Lord, please teach me the importance of today's quest so that I may be prepared for tomorrow.
Amen.

Chaplain Col. Kenneth N. Brown
Multi-National Corps-Iraq (MNC-I) Command Chaplain

A NEW WORLD

We pray, Father of all, who loves all men, for a new world wherein every race may be free, and government may be of the people, by all and for all, so that the nations, ordering their states wisely and worthily, may live in the example of your Son Jesus Christ our Lord, to whom with the Father and the Holy Spirit, may all the praise of the world be given, all power, dominion and glory for ever.
Amen.

Anonymous

GRATITUDE

God of all,
May you be praised! Eternity is full of your
glory! We, your people in uniform who serve
this nation, are grateful for your goodness,
your kindness, and your mercy. Accept our
thanksgiving and praise, eternal and righteous
God, as you continue to bless us and our
families with your presence. As we serve,
O God, may it be with valor, courage, and
integrity.

Keep our comrades safe in the combat zones.
Put a shield around them and help them to find
refuge in you when they are tired, and they feel
alone and far away. Strengthen their resolve
and bring them back safely to their families.

Bless and protect our families and loved ones who support us. Help them to remain confident of your persistent and watchful care for all service members. Accept our gratitude on behalf of all who serve on the home front and in the theaters of operations. We bless your holy and righteous name, now and always. Amen.

Chaplain Capt. Vincent J. Dominique
202nd MI BN Battalion Chaplain

FOR OUR COUNTRY'S FUTURE

Eternal Father, strong to save,
We are grateful for all your gifts, especially for
the liberty we enjoy. Thank you for freedom
from the tyranny of narrow-minded despots.
Thank you for liberty from the tyranny of
narrow-minded perspectives that oppress on
the basis of religion or race. Thank you for
those who defend our liberty. We pray for
sailors, marines, airmen, and soldiers, those
deployed and those serving at home. We pray
for the family members who serve in silence
and who make their missions possible. We
pray for those who have fallen in the struggle,
for the military personnel and civilians whose
blood waters the sea of liberty. We hold them
before you in these moments of silence…

Lord God, as the mission of liberty continues, we pray for those who lead. We ask extraordinary wisdom and courage for all in the chain of command, including our president and his advisors. We pray for our Congress that they may legislate wisely, and that all who lead our nation may depend on you and not on their own resources. Bless the United States of America, we humbly ask, and lead us in the ways that make for liberty and justice for all.

We ask this in your name.
Amen.

Chaplain Lt. Col. Mark E. Thompson
Deputy/Senior Clinician
EAMC DMPC

PRAYER FOR PEACE

I will both lie down and sleep in peace;
for you alone, O LORD, make me lie down in
safety.

Psalm 4:8

All powerful and ever-living God, we pray to
you to grant us peace.

We pray that you grant wisdom and courage to
our commanders and leaders, so that they seek
peaceful settlements to disputes before seeking
armed intervention.

We pray that you grant wisdom and courage to
the leaders of all nations, so that they will seek
to work together in harmony and peace.

We pray that you protect all the men and
women who so proudly serve our nation.
Keep them from harm, and give them tools
that they may find the strength to face the
daily challenges, and to pursue true peace and
justice. We pray that each soldier understands
that only peace brings true freedom.

When faced with the need to shed blood to preserve liberty, we seek your guidance, firm support, and your compassionate healing. Please protect us as we discharge our duties.

We pray that you protect our families and relatives, that they may find comfort as they await our safe return.

We ask these through Christ, our Lord. Amen.

Anonymous
Retired Lieutenant General
U.S. Air Force

ML   S/10